599.88
MAC   McDearmon, Kay

           Orangutans, the
           red apes

DATE DUE $8.95

Orangutans

ORANGUTANS

The Red Apes

Kay McDearmon

Illustrated with photographs

DODD, MEAD & COMPANY
New York

A SKYLIGHT BOOK

ACKNOWLEDGMENTS

I am grateful for the valuable assistance of Dr. Peter S. Rodman, anthropologist at the University of California, Davis, and for his photographs of orangutans taken in the field.
I would also like to thank Susan Hathaway, Photographic Librarian at the San Diego Zoo, for her special efforts to secure additional photographs.

PICTURE CREDITS

Dr. Peter S. Rodman, 8, 14, 15, 16, 22, 31, 37, 39, 60; Heidi Schroeder, 11; © Zoological Society of San Diego, 19, 23, 24, 27, 32, 35, 42, 44, 46, 48, 51, 54, 58.

Library of Congress Cataloging in Publication Data

McDearmon, Kay.
Orangutans, the red apes.

(A Skylight book)
Includes index.
Summary: Discusses the habitat, physical character-
istics, lifestyle, and feeding and mating habits of
orangutans, with chapters on their history, legends, and
life in the zoo.
1. Orangutan—Juvenile literature.   [1. Orangutan]
I. Title.
QL737.P96M4   1983   599.88'42   83-8950
ISBN 0-396-08182-7

To Pam and Jackie

Contents

1

Meet the Orangutan

One drizzly day in the Asian rain forest a shaggy red ape was resting in its leafy nest high in a fig tree. When it heard rustling below, the curious orangutan peered over the edge of its nest. It saw a man standing upon the forest floor watching it.

To chase him away, the orangutan climbed to the top of the tree and shook it vigorously several times. Then the animal tore off a few branches and tossed them to the ground. When the scientist didn't leave, the red ape quietly climbed away through the trees.

A fully grown male orangutan holding onto a tree limb in the jungle.

Another day a huge male orangutan, walking on all fours in the Borneo jungle, was startled when the brush parted and a human face appeared through it. For a moment orang and scientist stared at each other, face to face. Then the red ape quickly climbed up into the closest tree. That was all.

Events such as these tend to prove the long-held belief that the orangutan is mild and retiring, and will not attack man unless it is provoked. Yet the red ape could easily overcome an unarmed man, as it is several times stronger. And tribal chiefs have claimed that the orangutan can even kill the fearsome crocodile.

Certainly the full-grown male orangutan can look frightening. He may weigh two hundred pounds—as much as a large man—but with long, thick hair flowing over his head and shoulders like a huge cape, he looks much larger than he really is.

A long beard, a mustache, fat cheek pads that almost

A zoo orangutan using all four feet, which resemble hands, for grasping.

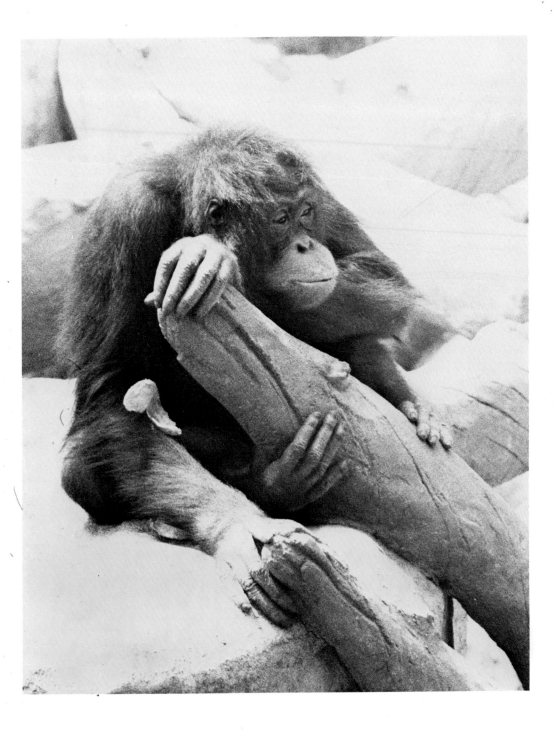

circle his face, and a throat sac that the animal can blow up like a balloon add to the effect. And his extremely long, powerful arms, outstretched, can measure eight feet from fingertip to fingertip.

The orangutan (*Pongo pygmaeus*), like man himself, is a primate. This is the highest order in the animal kingdom. Altogether, it includes about two hundred kinds of mammals, mostly tree-living.

Primates differ from other mammals in various ways. All primates have movable fingers, with nails instead of claws, giving them better grasping ability. With eyes set in front of their heads, they can view objects with both eyes at once. This allows them to judge distance.

Apes are the highest primates next to man. The orangutan is one of the Great Apes, a group that includes gorillas and chimpanzees.

2

Its Home in the Rain Forest

Long ago orangutans thrived in dense forests from South China to Java. Now they live only in remote jungle areas on the islands of Borneo and Sumatra. Some trees there tower 250 feet above the forest floor. Orangs live in trees that are from twenty to seventy feet high.

The rain forest is home for a rich mixture of animal life. There's a small mouse deer only one foot high; giant ants that bite and squirt acid from their rears; and bats with five-foot wings that sleep upside down during the day and fly around the jungle at night sampling the fruit.

Borneo's forest shelters not only flying squirrels, but also flying tree frogs, tree snakes, and lizards. In spite of their names, these animals really glide, rather than fly. The frog's webbed feet expand and cushion its landing. The lizard's skin-covered ribs open like a fan, and act like motionless wings. And the snake flattens its ribs as it leaps off the end of a branch.

A ground view of the rain forest taken in the early morning when the mist was still rising from the vegetation.

A tree full of fruit bats sleeping together in the early morning.

A slow loris. It lives in the highest layer of the jungle trees, a layer or so higher than the orangutan.

With so much animal life around there is always noise. Insects hum, tropical birds chirp, monkeys call, and gibbons hoot and sing. At times orangutans add their squeaks and howls to the chorus.

Their dark jungle home is warm and humid all year round. Moist winds, called monsoons, drop over one hundred inches of rain in a single year.

Plants grow in greater variety there than anywhere else on earth. Much of the year, too, wild flowers bloom. Most unusual is the enormous rafflesia that measures over two feet across. And eight hundred kinds of tiny orchids add their delicate beauty to the forest scene.

3

Legends and History

Over the years natives of Southeast Asia have told various tales about the origin of their "man of the forest," the orangutan.

One ancient story claimed that one day their bird gods created a man and a woman. They were so pleased with themselves that they held a great feast. Afterward, they tried to create more people. But they had forgotten just how they did it, and the result was the first orangutan.

For other natives the fiery-colored apes were people who had angered the gods. To punish them, they covered the wicked men with long red fur and banished them forever into the forest.

A full-grown male orangutan, with long red fur.

Orangutans have been on this earth for a really long time. Archaeologists, digging in a giant cave in Borneo, found that these Great Apes existed 35,000 years ago in the early Stone Age. Their charred bones also reveal that they were a favorite item on the menu of cavemen.

From ancient times orangutans also have been hunted for pets. Natives preferred the more appealing infants. To capture them tribal hunters first speared their ever-present mothers.

Explorers brought little orangs to Europe about a hundred years ago as gifts to princes. They found the red apes amusing. Years after, zoos began to buy them. Sadly, only about half of those shipped overseas survived the voyage.

4
Daily Life

Orangutans travel mostly through the trees in the rain forest. As they reach out with their long arms and swing from branch to branch, their fingers and toes act like hooks for grasping. Like trapeze artists, they can hang upside down and swing their bodies in all directions.

They move slowly from one fruit tree to another, the heavier animals testing branches as they travel along. Yet orangutans sometimes fall.

The lucky ones land in trees on the way down or catch themselves on branches. The others crash to the forest floor, and can end up with broken bones. One day a

An orangutan climbing a tree in the rain forest.

scientist in Borneo observed Rinnie, a little red ape, grab a rotten vine, tumble to the earth, and break her arm.

Because their legs are much shorter and weaker than their arms, it is awkward for orangs to walk, either on all

Mature, but not yet fully grown, a male orangutan stretches his long arms.

Orangutans like to put almost anything on their heads. This full-grown female seems to enjoy putting on a "hat."

fours or upright. But when the older, heavier males find it hard to locate vines or branches that will support them, they may travel on the ground. At times an animal may leave the treetops to visit a natural salt lick to get the salt missing from its diet.

Orangutans like water, and if they need to cross a river, they will wade in it up to their hips. But they can't swim, and when the water gets too deep for them, they try to grab rides on fallen logs.

At home in the jungle, orangutans build nests in the trees by bending branches and folding them together to form platforms. They take naps in their springy nests during the day. When it rains they pile leaves above the nests to act as roofs. Or they may hold leafy branches up above their heads, umbrella-like.

About sunset when they retire, most orangs build fresh nests. Now and then a full-grown male may choose to sleep on the forest floor, perhaps in a nest built on fallen logs.

Orangutans are early risers. They begin their day by swinging to the fruit trees they visited last the day before, and eating hearty breakfasts. Afterward, as they travel from tree to tree, they often stop to snack or to rest. They enjoy their longest nap in midday, and their longest feast near the afternoon's end.

Unlike many other apes and monkeys, orangutans rarely groom each other. Orangs are not really social animals—like most other primates—and actually spend more time alone than in groups of any kind.

Full-grown males almost always travel alone, and younger males also travel by themselves much of the time. They avoid the older males, and flee when they appear.

One day a young male orang, called Mute by the scientist observing him, was wandering alone in the dank Borneo rain forest when he spied a wet log on the ground. Breaking off a branch, he began examining it for termites. Suddenly, he looked up and saw Nick, a huge older male, dining on termites at the other end. Mute quickly dropped the branch and scooted off on all fours.

Mothers are more social. They often travel through the evergreens with one or two little orangs. But years later, after the youngster has grown up, if it should meet its

A quiet gibbon family scene. Like most primates, these apes live in groups.

mother in the jungle, the two will act like strangers.

Living rather solitary lives seems to work well for the red apes. If they lived and traveled in large groups with full-grown males and females like gorillas, for example, they would have trouble finding enough to eat.

The heavier males, which need much more food, could strip a fruit tree in a day or two, leaving the others too little to eat. As these males also move more slowly, they would hold the others back as well.

But as orangutans travel singly, or nearly so, each male can move at its own pace, while the lighter orangs can travel farther and faster. This way they can find more food and have more choices.

5

What the Orangutan Eats

While gorillas are herbivores, or plant-eaters, the orangutan is the largest-bodied, fruit-eating animal in the world. As such it needs a large amount of fruit, and spends many of its waking hours hunting for it. But finding its favorite fruit trees isn't easy.

Trees of the same kind are widely scattered. In any one place trees bear fruit at different times—some as often as every few months, some as seldom as every four years. So an orang may have to search far for the fruit it favors, and to rely on its memory as to when and where to find it.

A scientist once observed a young male in the Borneo forest that seemed to do this very well. When wild plums began to ripen, he traveled directly from one plum tree to another, visiting six in one day, even though he hadn't been in the area for some time.

An orangutan stuffs itself with fruit when it is plentiful, and often has to compete for it with other tree-living animals in the jungle. Any fig tree it locates, for example, may already be occupied by gibbons, monkeys, and squirrels—all gorging themselves on figs.

While the red ape sometimes dines on figs, its favorite fruit is the football-sized durian. With its large, shovel-shaped front teeth and powerful hands the orang rips open the thick, thorny rind to get at the delicious pulp. Some people say it tastes like butter almond ice-cream.

The pulp smells like rotting onions, but natives share the animal's liking for durians. They are a luxury in China, and a famous naturalist once claimed that it was worth a trip to Southeast Asia just to dine on durians.

A fully grown male orangutan feeding on the fruit of a Seng Kuan tree in Borneo.

Another fruit that the orang especially likes is the globe-shaped banitan. But before it can enjoy the sweet, coconut-like meat, the great ape must open two pits so hard they won't yield to a nutcracker. Only a grown orangutan can open the pits and it spends hours crushing them with its teeth.

On its daily rounds, and especially when fruit is scarce, the red ape chews on bark and nibbles on leaves, ferns, flowers, and buds. Now and then it eats birds' eggs and snacks on insects. It digs up ground nests of termites with its bare hands, and scoops up the juicy insects. For a special treat the orangutan may add an occasional lizard to its diet.

When an orang is thirsty it licks water off the wet leaves in its nest. When traveling, the red ape plunges a hand into a hole in a tree trunk where water has gathered, withdraws its hand, and then licks its damp fur.

A proboscis monkey and baby. These long-nosed monkeys are found only in Borneo and are becoming increasingly rare.

6

Birth and Infancy

Orangutan babies can be born at any time of the year. A single baby is usual, but a mother at the Seattle Zoo once gave birth to twins.

Only once has a birth been seen in the wild. When a scientist noticed that an orangutan living near her Borneo camp was pregnant, she followed her, hoping to observe the birth. Each night for a month she slept underneath the tree in which Fern, the mother-to-be, nested. Then one day the scientist saw Fern suddenly stop feeding and

Mother with new baby—close as always.

build a new nest. There, seventy feet above the forest floor, the baby was born.

The next day Biruté Galdikas, the scientist, saw the little orang in its mother's arms, and later reported that it probably weighed slightly over two pounds at birth.

The newborn orangutan is covered with orange fur, and wisps of it frame its dark humanlike face. Helpless at first, the tiny infant clings to its mother's long hair. Like a human baby, it sleeps most of the time, awakening only to sample her warm milk.

While the infant is awake, its mother exercises its little arms and legs. Before long she gently pulls her baby around the nest on its tummy to coax it to crawl. At times she grooms her baby's coat. Now and then she tickles and plays with her infant, and sometimes she lifts her newborn baby onto her head.

All during its first year whenever its mother leaves her nest, the baby goes along, holding tightly onto its mother's

Mother with her male youngster. He now requires much less carrying than when he was an infant.

side or back as she swings through the trees. As she eats, she sometimes stuffs pieces of prechewed food into her baby's mouth.

By its first birthday the infant weighs about fifteen pounds. Now the little orang nibbles on bits of food its mother drops on her fur. The mother begins to share some of her meals with her infant, but she doesn't always give her baby as much food as it wants.

Once when a mother kept biting into one mango after another without offering any of the fruit to her infant, it screamed loud and long. The mother ignored its temper tantrum. But when the baby quieted down, she handed it a mango.

A mother's love of wild honey may also cause her to ignore her baby for a short time. This happens rarely because bees nest near the tops of high trees with bare trunks that orangs can't climb. But one day a leathery-faced mother, her infant on her back, saw a bee tree that sun bears had visited. The grooves they had clawed in the trunk allowed her to climb to the top. Once she attacked the honeycomb, angry bees swarmed over her. Surpris-

A three-year-old orangutan enjoying a hiding place.

ingly, she just kept eating the honey, paying no attention to the bees or her baby!

Back in the nest, while its mother naps, the infant sometimes amuses itself by tossing leaves around or bending branches together to make a play nest. Then one day its mother pushes her little one out on a branch to teach it how to climb. Soon it is swinging from branch to branch like an acrobat.

As the months go by, the small orang depends less and less upon its mother. When they travel together, the infant begins to choose its own fruit. As it eats more food each day, it nurses less.

7

Growing Up

A two-year-old orangutan is no longer an infant, but its mother will still allow it to nurse at times, perhaps for a few years more. Meanwhile, the youngster continues to share its mother's nest at night, but it sometimes takes daytime naps in a nest it has built for itself.

Unlike other Great Apes that have a choice of playmates within their living group, a young orangutan rarely gets a chance to play with others of its own age. This happens only when their mothers meet in the jungle, and they all travel together for a day or two.

During an orang's third year it may wander off alone to search for a playmate. If it finds another orangutan, they chase through the trees, wrestle, and playfully bite

A young orangutan watching intently.

each other's fingers, toes, and neck. While staying close together, at times they play separately, swinging from limbs, somersaulting, and piling branches over their heads. These play sessions usually break up after a short while.

An orang will be at least four years old before its mother mates again. When she does mate, the pair may travel together and sleep in the same tree for a few days or weeks. Then the male disappears. Nine months later the new baby is born.

At this time the mother pushes her firstborn out of the nest. This may so anger the youngster that it flings its arms and legs around and screams, throwing a temper tantrum. The orang may try several times to return to the nest, but its mother will not allow it to enter.

Though her youngster can't share his mother's nest any longer, a male continues to accompany its mother and her new infant for awhile. Then he roams through the rain forest until he finds a new living area for himself far away from his first one.

A female orang forced out of its mother's nest usually travels with her mother as much as a year longer than a

A young male exploring the inside of a ball.

male. By watching her care for the new baby, the growing female learns skills she will need when she takes care of her own infant. When she does leave her mother's home range, she will search for a place close by to live. Her new home will overlap her mother's home range.

While a male orangutan feeds and travels within an area of about two square miles, a female lives within a much smaller area. Unlike gibbons, an orang at times leaves its home range. For example, it may wander to a riverbank on a winter's day when there is no food, and nibble on young shoots growing close to the water.

A female orangutan is mature at seven years of age, but she may delay accepting a mate until she is almost full grown, about three years later. Then she will be about 3½ feet tall, and weigh one hundred pounds at most.

When a male orang is ten years old, he is mature and can mate. But females seem to prefer shaggy-haired, full-grown males that are about 4½ feet tall, between twelve and fifteen years old, and weighing as much as two hundred pounds.

Red apes vary as much in appearance as people do. Be-

A female orangutan snarling at a male.

sides differing in size, they differ in the shape of their faces and length of their hair. And an older animal may have chocolate or almost black hair.

Mature males of any age avoid contact with each other. When a male wants to announce his claim to a location and send any males visiting in the area scurrying off, he gives a frightening "long call." Sometimes he also shakes branches and hurls a few earthward. But orangutans rarely fight.

Yet two mature males may fight over a female. One such struggle began high in a tree in Borneo. The males bit each other on the face, hands, and shoulders. Then they chased through the branches. When they fell to the ground, they climbed back into the trees and fought again. Finally, some thirty minutes later, the stranger vanished, and the winning male rejoined the female he was courting.

No one knows how long red apes live in the wild. Experts say the luckiest may live from twenty-five to forty years. In zoos they sometimes live longer. Guarina, a Philadelphia Zoo orangutan, lived fifty-seven years, setting a world record.

47

8

Life in the Zoo

Many of the first orangutans shipped overseas to zoos lived only a few months. Until they learned how to feed them, zoos had a hard time just keeping them alive. Over the years they have worked out diets that keep their red apes well nourished and trim.

At first zoos thought orangutans could be kept in cages. But, bored by their bare quarters, they soon became "escape artists." One strong male at the San Diego Zoo untwisted the wires of his cage and pushed himself through the opening. Transferred to a stronger cage, he escaped

Bob—the "escape artist."

again. Then a third cage was provided for him. This one had held lions and grizzlies, but it couldn't hold young Bob!

The more fortunate zoo orangs now live in outdoor junglelike areas. But instead of climbing around his home, a large male may use his remarkable strength to destroy it. A full-grown Bronx Zoo orangutan twisted metal cables and loosened imitation branches that were bolted to the wall. And he tore up a metal grill to get a grape that had dropped into it.

Zoos faced still other problems. Like other Great Apes, orangutans easily catch human diseases such as polio, pneumonia, and malaria. They may also choke on food or objects tossed to them by visitors. The more modern zoos now surround their orangutans' homes with glass to protect them from germs and from visitors. Of course, when red apes become ill, zoos provide medical treatment.

Overall, zoos have done well in improving early conditions. Now orangutans are staying alive much longer, and more are having babies.

In their newer quarters little orangs play—together and

50

A female infant resting quietly in the zoo.

alone—much as they do in the wild. They also enjoy playing in water, and at times older males take long baths.

Many youngsters have learned new tricks. When a photographer appears, they perform handstands to catch his attention. For a show at the Bronx Zoo orangs rode tricycles. And in Las Vegas, performing along with a few chimpanzees, orangutans danced the hula on a drum.

9

Language and Intelligence

Orangutans are quiet animals compared with their noisy cousins, the chimpanzees. But orangs also make a variety of sounds—including grunts, barks, squeaks, and screams.

Mature males also balloon out their throat sacs and emit "long calls"—a series of groans and roars that can last four minutes and be heard for a mile.

All their sounds convey meaning to orangutans, but experts say there's a giant gap between those sounds and real language. If you believe an old legend, the red apes could speak, but feared if they did, someone would put them to work!

Two attempts have been made to get captive orangs to

A full-grown male orangutan. Note the large throat sac.

54

speak. They were hardly encouraging. After a year of daily lessons, Cody—an infant and the best performer—could only say four words clearly. Still, this was better than the chimpanzee, Viki, who took six years to learn to speak four words.

Captive apes have done much better learning Ameslan—the sign language used in the United States. Washoe, the first and most famous chimpanzee student, mastered 160 signs in five years, and used them in combinations. Koko, a gorilla, has been learning signs the last several years at about the same rate as Washoe and seems to use them as well.

Recently scientists in Borneo have been teaching orang-utans to use signs. This is the first time anyone has tried to teach any of the Great Apes sign language in the wild. After one year Princess is "talking" as well as Washoe and Koko did in a similar period.

Early tests of the abilities of captive apes—most of them lively chimpanzees—suggested that they were the "whiz kids of the Great Apes." But observers of the quiet, slow-moving orangutan have since had some surprises.

Instead of just using the stick testers left it to reach for a banana, one orang climbed upon the long stick and used it as a vaulting pole. Another made a swing for itself by gathering the straw in its cage, fashioning it into a rope, and hanging it over his door.

Orangutans can tie knots and they have no trouble opening childproof medicine bottles. They can even choose the correct key from a group in order to open doors. They use objects as tools to widen the bars of their cages and escape. One red ape used a piece of metal from his trapeze.

Experts claimed some time ago that there is little difference in the intelligence of the three Great Apes. But they said that the orang is the best tool-user. Now the latest studies suggest that red apes may be just a bit brainier than chimpanzees.

10

Future of the Orangutan

Living high in the trees, as orangutans do most of their days, they have no natural enemies. While a clouded leopard might grab a young orang traveling alone, this cat is too small to be a regular predator. Even in Sumatra where tigers and larger leopards live, they prey on wild pigs and deer that roam about the forest floor and are much easier to catch.

As is the case with the other Great Apes, man is the orangutan's greatest enemy.

Experts worry that the orangutan will die out in the wild—and for good reason. Once, long ago, there were hundreds of thousands; now only a few thousand remain.

A clouded leopard—a possible but unlikely orangutan enemy.

A leading scientist says they are the most endangered of the Great Apes.

Certainly today the orangs are still disappearing at an alarming rate. Tribes in remote areas of Borneo hunt them for food. Smugglers break the law by capturing and selling them for the high prices they bring. Recently in California, for example, an orangutan sold for $10,000.

Orangutans are also slow to recover their losses in the wild. Females give birth to only a single offspring at a time, and there are several years between births.

Loggers are the greatest threat to the red apes' survival. They are fast cutting down trees to provide land and lumber for farms for the growing population. So more and more orangs are losing their forest homes, and must find others if they are to survive.

Efforts are being made to save the orangutan in the wild. Special areas have been set aside for them in the jungle. Local laws against hunting them are now being more strictly enforced, and pet owners are being required to give up their orangs.

Scientists in Borneo and Sumatra have been teaching

59

rescued pets and orphan orangutans how to live and survive in the wild. It hasn't been easy—some pets are terrified of climbing! But some orangs have been successfully returned to the special areas reserved for them in the wild.

At present zoos may offer the best hope of saving the orangutans, as they are giving special attention to breeding and raising little ones. Zoos and laboratories now pair their orangs—putting one male and one female together. They also exchange animals to try to breed more babies. And when a captive mother rejects its baby, the zoo tries to find another orang to act as a foster mother.

All the efforts being made in zoos and in the wild to save the remarkable red ape must succeed. As one scientist recently said, "We have learned much about orangutans. We certainly know better than to lose them."

Edie, a female orphan brought to a scientist's camp in Borneo. There Dr. Rodman cared for her and helped her learn the ways of the wild. She now lives free in the forest.

Index